Pebble® Plus

MAKE IT MINE

Kid Style

BOSS BACKPACKS FOR YOU!

by Megan Cooley Peterson

Consulting editor: Gail Saunders-Smith, PhD

CAPSTONE PRESS
a capstone imprint

Pebble Plus is published by Capstone Press,
1710 Roe Crest Drive, North Mankato, Minnesota 56003
www.capstonepub.com

Library of Congress Cataloging-in-Publication Data
Peterson, Megan Cooley,
Kid style. Boss backpacks for you! / by Megan Cooley Peterson.
pages cm.—(Pebble plus. Make it mine)
Summary: "Full-color photographs and simple text provide easy
ways to personalize a backpack"—Provided by publisher.
Audience: 5–8.
Audience: Grade K to 3.
Includes bibliographical references.
ISBN 978-1-4765-3969-0 (library binding)
ISBN 978-1-4765-6032-8 (eBook pdf)
1. Backpacks—Juvenile literature. 2. Handicraft—Juvenile literature.
3. Decoration and ornament—Juvenile literature. I. Title. II.
Title: Boss backpacks for you!
TT649.P48 2013
646.4'8—dc23   2013035762

Editorial Credits
Jeni Wittrock, editor; Tracy Davies McCabe, designer; Svetlana Zhurkin,
media researcher; Jennifer Walker, production specialist; Sarah Schuette,
photo stylist; Marcy Morin, photo scheduler

Photo Credits
All photos by Capstone Studio/Karon Dubke

Printed in the United States of America in North Mankato, Minnesota.
092013   007775CGS14

TABLE OF CONTENTS

Backpack Fun

Carry your stuff in style in a backpack you decorated yourself! Wow your friends with easy-to-make projects.

You can find some supplies
around the house.
The rest can be bought
at a craft store.

Basic Tools List:

- duct tape
- scissors
- craft foam
- hole punch
- ribbon
- fabric markers
- 3-D paint
- acrylic paint
- paintbrush
- modeling clay
- chenille stems
- fabric
- decoupage glue

Duct Tape Straps

Give your backpack new life
with colorful duct tape.
Wrap each strap with tape.
Peel off the tape when
you're ready for a new look.

Bag Tag

Move to the head of the class with a one-of-a-kind bag tag. First cut out a tag from craft foam.

Punch a hole at the top of the tag with a hole punch. Dress up your tag with stickers and paint.

Loop ribbon through the hole. Tie your tag to a zipper on your backpack.

Backpack Art

Carry your books to school in a work of art. Use fabric markers and 3-D paint to give your bag a pop of color.

Paint Splash

Bored with your backpack?
Splatter it with different
colors of paint!
Do this project outside
and on newspapers.

Custom Zipper Pulls

Anyone can buy zipper pulls at the store. It's more fun to make your own! To begin, mold modeling clay into different shapes.

Use a toothpick to poke holes in the tops of your zipper pulls. Let dry. Slip chenille stems through the holes. Then attach them to your backpack zippers.

Take It to the Next Level

Take your backpack to the next
level with fabric and beads.
Follow these steps or make your
own creation. Make sure to ask
an adult to help you.

Step 1: Cut fabric scraps into different shapes and sizes.

Step 2: Using a foam brush, paint fabric decoupage glue on a small area of your backpack.

Step 3: Place a piece of fabric over the glue. Press down with your fingers to smooth the fabric.

Step 4: Repeat steps 2 and 3 until the bag is covered. Let it dry.

Step 5: Paint a layer of decoupage glue over the top of the fabric. Let it dry.

Step 6: Ask an adult to hot glue beads or small toys to your backpack.

Read More

Kenney, Karen Latchana. *Super Simple Art to Wear: Fun and Easy-to-Make Crafts for Kids.* Super Simple Crafts. Edina, Minn.: ABDO Pub. Company, 2010.

Laughlin, Kara L. *Beautiful Bags for the Crafty Fashionista.* Fashion Craft Studio. Mankato, Minn.: Capstone Press, 2012.

Wrigley, Annabel. *We Love to Sew: 28 Pretty Things to Make: Jewelry, Headbands, Softies, T-shirts, Pillows, Bags, & More.* Lafayette, Calif.: C & T Publishing, 2013.

Internet Sites

FactHound offers a safe, fun way to find Internet sites related to this book. All of the sites on FactHound have been researched by our staff.

Here's all you do:

Visit *www.facthound.com*

Type in this code: 9781476539690

Check out projects, games and lots more at
www.capstonekids.com

24

Word Count: 206
Grade: 1
Early-Intervention Level: 18